# Breaking into Phonics

An interactive workbook for parents and children.

Patrice Barrett

I

# Breaking into Phonics

# By Patrice Barrett

Copyright © 2018 by Patrice Barrett
All rights reserved. This book or any portion thereof
may not be reproduced or used in any manner whatsoever
without the express written permission of the author
except for the use of brief quotations in a book review.

First Printing, 2018

ISBN 978-0-692-10560-3

Publisher: ClassroomsAtHome, LLC
Front Cover Design: B* Creatives
Back Cover Design: Morton Works Production
Editor: Julia Johnson and Heather K.

Distributor: Lulu Press
627 Davis Dr. Suite 300,
Morrisville, NC 27560

This page is intentionally left blank.

# Table of Contents

What is Reading?............................................................................1

Reading Skills and High School: The Relationship..........................3

Importance of Nonfiction...............................................................5

Rules for Using this Text Effectively...............................................6

Daily Suggested Routines after Completing the Initial Worksheet......9

Spelling Rule Calendar.................................................................11

Introduction Sounds....................................................................12

Meet Vowel Diagraphs.................................................................27

Meet Diphthongs.........................................................................31

Can You Score With Me?..............................................................32

Meet Vowel Teams .....................................................................34

Meet the Friendly Team...............................................................40

Meet the Tricky Team..................................................................41

Consonant Clusters.....................................................................42

Game Time.................................................................................44

What is Meaning?........................................................................47

What is Writing?..........................................................................54

Bibliography................................................................................61

This page is intentionally left blank.

# What Is Reading?

When discussing reading we cannot leave out the concept of language. What is language? What is its purpose? According to Dennis O'Neil (2006), language is a set of rules for generating speech.

Language is the order of words compiled together in order to create an understanding. So, if our definition of language is something people have to interpret, we must be able to read those marks on the page in order for language to be effective. So, is reading just a bunch of words on a page? In a way, yes it is! **However, before you can make sense of various words, you must be able to make sense of sounds and the appropriate letter associated with said sound.** Each letter has the capacity to make one or more sounds depending on the placement of the letter in the word. A reader must be able to comprehend that *[r]* makes the *'rrrrr'* sound and *[a]* makes the *'aahhh'* sound and *[t]* makes a sharp *'tuh'* sound. A reader must know what the sounds represent and like an equation they must be able to *"solve"* all of the letters in each word. Therefore, there must be multiple approaches in order for a reader to make sense of any written language. What a reader does first is take in the letters. They assume the sounds it makes; they bring in memories they've had with these letters, and then they experiment with the sound. Thus, a reader accesses knowledge and past experiences, and they pull out a strategy to make sense of the visual markings (letters). Who said reading was easy? [I know it all may sound complex, but a reader has to sort through all these processes as they read!](#)

This is where the work comes in. If our students are able to become strong phonetic detectives who can comprehend various words with ease then we set our students up to be both successful and resourceful readers. **Reading is having the ability to understand marks (letters) on a page and gain understanding and meaning from those marks.** We want our students to not only be able to read, but understand what they're reading!

# Reading Skills & High School: The Relationship

There is a saying that "prisons are built based on the amount of 3rd graders reading below grade level." It's a harsh claim; however, *students who do not read on grade level in the early years are 4 times more likely to drop out compared to their counterparts* (Reading Partners, 2013). Many studies have followed third graders, who read below grade level. It's proven that only a handful of these students catch up academically. What happens to a third grader who get passed along from grade to grade and enters **high school** still reading on a third-grade level? Ask yourself that question. The likelihood that these students catch up is low according to data.

We must ask ourselves how to keep this from happening. There is a gap in student achievement and we must work together to analyze data and provide intense instruction to our children and our students.

A lack of academic achievement is the key reason students drop out of high school according to RIF stats and literacy facts. **High school dropouts commit about 75% of crimes in the U.S.**

(Krache, 2012). Can we assume that weaknesses in reading skills severely impact the high school dropout rate? This in turn impacts the amount of people we have wasting potential in prison cells. Think about this: how often are new high schools being constructed versus how often new prisons are being constructed? I would like to think if we can bridge the gap between nonreaders and readers, then we can perhaps decrease the amount of people we have in prison. I am nowhere near a politician, but with the hopes of touching various children's reading skills we will catch our students who are left behind.

# Importance of Nonfiction

What is nonfiction? To some, it may be the boring books we read about with stuff we do not like! To others, *nonfiction books can be identified as text created to inform individuals on information on specific topics.* It's imperative for our young children to read nonfiction because it gives them more knowledge. Knowledge leads to opinions and opinions leads to our students becoming actual doers. Nonfiction also bridges the gap between the experiences of our students and students from other regions. Why is this important? Did you know most reading assessments that are created are geared toward children with a common experience in mind? But how does one level the playing field for their young reader if their experiences don't fall under a certain category? By reading nonfiction books weekly. Nonfiction allows all students to learn about other readers, characters, and gives everyone a common playing field without ever leaving one's library.

# Rules for Using this Text Effectively

- Children are not expected to read and carry out expectations independently.
    - Please assist the child with this text.
- The student tasks are included and should be completed with assistance at all times!
- These suggestions are all geared toward helping our students have a stronger reading foundation.
    - Please approach each suggestion with an open mind.
- You can purchase a child's thesaurus or spend time reading one at a local library. Find 2 new "big" words and practice using them throughout the week. Let's treat it like studying for the SAT's.
- We want our children to be able to name items with multiple names. This is the purpose of having a thesaurus. We want our students to be prepared in case they encounter new vocabulary on standardized testing. If we build students background knowledge and experiences with words and

meanings, they should be able to navigate new terminology with confidence.

- o For example, ask your child what do we call milk jugs? Cartons? Containers?
- o What about bed spreads? Do some people call them comforters?
- o What about your dresser that houses your clothing? What other names do people call them?

**I'm asking that you read at least 3 nonfiction books a week with your child. Two of the books should be on your child's grade level. *Ask the librarian for assistance. Read the challenging books to your child during family time.**

Ask the following target questions:

1. What did you learn in this book?

    Suggested response: *I learned that fish can weigh different amounts.*

2. Would you write a book like this?

Suggested response: *I would write a book like this, but I would change it to a picture book. This book needs more pictures to help people make sense about building cars.*

3. What did you notice about how this book was written?

   Suggested response: *I noticed the author kept saying the word 'habitat' on each page. I also noticed there were some bold words. They helped me pay close attention to the pictures.*

4. Did it make sense to you?

   Suggested response: *No, this book didn't make sense. The words were too hard. Or…This book made sense because I already learned about ponds. This book just helped me make more connections about ponds, lakes, and oceans.*

5. Could you write a fiction book about this topic? *Try it!*

Suggested Materials

- Composition Notebooks -**Required**
- Pencils, Pens and Highlighters
- Construction paper
- Tape
- Index Cards- students can write words or sounds of the day on these index cards and "study" them throughout the week and then glue them in their journal
- Small to medium sized posters – students will create mini book reports or projects
- Dry erase boards- use as needed

# Daily Suggested Routines after Completing the Initial Worksheet

Different activities spread over the course of the week...

- Write and search.
    - Write a sentence with each spelling rule or sound of the week on a blank page. Your job is to find 7 more of those words in a brand-new book! Write each one on an index card. After that you can take another spelling rule of the day and write it into your journal with two examples. You can write one word on an index card and place that index card next to your favorite item. Practice saying and spelling that word for a few days.
- Spot the word.
    - Find the spelling rule or sound of the week word in a nonfiction book after you read it. Read it to a new family in person or through video chat. Teach your family member or friend what the rule says and give them

examples to spell out. You can demonstrate your word from your dry erase board or your notebook.

*All notebooks should be kept as neat as possible in case the student decides to use it for a demonstration.

- Quiz Day (Optional)
    - Practice saying the new words and sound out each word. Take a spelling quiz based on the rules you learned this week. Place the quiz at the back of the notebook.
    - Grading the quiz is optional.

*Disclaimer: The purpose of this book is to teach multiple sounds of various letters. Each spelling rule will **not** be applicable to all words. This means that the "appropriate sound" will only work most of the time. For example, the "magic e" occurs at the end of a word. However, every e is not a "magic e." Certain rules apply, such as the previous vowel must become a long vowel as in "like." If we look at the word puzzle, we notice it does have an "e" at the end. However, this is not what we call a "magic e". The previous vowel (u) is not a long vowel. Once again, all words that end in e are not considered magic e.*

Record notes and ideas below (parent or student):

You can use a space like this if thoughts or aha moments come to mind. You can also use this space if you do not have a journal nearby. The purpose of this space is to jot down important ideas, conclusions, or pictures that demonstrate understanding. It is my hope that during a weekend "review" the notes will trigger memories for specific sounds and increase a student's understanding for the topic.

# Spelling Rule Calendar

**I would like you to work on one spelling rule or sound each week.**

The structure of the book is intended for a cycle of activities. For example, each spelling rule or sound has an activity page. You may do that entire page in one or two days. There are also suggested routines for interacting with the spelling rule or sound you have worked on for the week. You may choose to do a rotation of various activities as listed below:

Day 1: Activity within the workbook

Day 2: Write and search

Day 3: Spot the word

Day 4: Variation including:

- Quiz Day (optional)

- Write a poem using the spelling rule of the week. Add three pictures to support your poem!

- Teach a spelling rule to another child. Have fun being the teacher!

The songs/poems can be used in order or used during a weekend review.

Once you have been through each spelling rule, I ask that you review any rule occasionally on a weekend (10 minutes max).

- Please sing any poem to the tune that works for you.
- The children should use hand motions to accompany their song. You can review any sound using videos from the internet, the composition journal or this work book. I suggest using all 3 resources weekly. Allow the student to lead the demonstration or review.

# OA sounds like OOOOOOO!!

Song 1
 O-A says o o o o o o.
That is a long o sound.
 Song 2
O-A makes the O sound
O-A makes the O sound
(pause for 3) goat (1-2) boat (1-2) soap (1-2) coat

# AI sounds like AAAAAA!!

Chant: Drum Rolllll
Person 1: Who is that?
Person 2: It's A and I
Person 1: Who?
Person: It's A and I!  We make the long A sound. Listen up!
 (pause for 3) rain (1-2) pain (1-2) pail (1-2) snail

# EA sounds like EEEEEEE!!

Mr. E-A was having a very bad day
His friends just didn't know what to say
One by one they carved words in a tree
Mr. E-A didn't know what he would see.
As he got closer he took a look
There were words he could use in a book!
Words that sounded like long E words.
And this is what he heard
(pause) Leader (1- 2) Leaf (1 -2) Dream (1 -2) Speak

# Q-U sounds like /kw/ or qughhhh!!

Song 1
Q-U says qu, qu, qu... Q-U says qu, qu, qu.
Song 2
Q-U on that quiz - qu!
Q-U on that quote - qu!
Q-U on that queen - qu!
Q-U on that question - qu!
Q-U on that squeeze - qu!


# IE sounds like IIIIII!!

I and E go walking
I and E go walking
I and E go walking
I and E go walking, but "I" does all the talking.
(1-2-3) pie (1-2-3) lie (1-2-3) tie (1-2-3) fries (1-2-3) spied
(1-2-3) dried

# EE sounds like EEEEEE!!

There was a bee!
Who lived in a tree!
And all he could see
Were the words in his tree
Clap Clap
Ee says eeeeeee
Clap Clap  peep (clap) jeep (clap) deep (clap) creek (clap)sheep!
Ee says eeeee!!

# OW/OU sounds like OUCHHHH!!

Oww oh yeah goes at the end like cow!
Ouu oh yeah goes in the middle like house!
Owww oh yeah goes at the end like how!
Ouu oh yeah goes in the middle like sound!
Oww  oh yea ouu (sounds like ow)
owww  oh yeah ouuu
Cloud - O U
Growl - O W
Shout - O U
Clown - O W

# C is my GUYYYYY!!

You don't want no problems with c
You don't want no problems with c
Meet my friend c
He always knows which way to be
C sounds like an S
If it's in front of an E, I, or Y
But it's not time for him to rest
C is still my guy!
City! Cent! Circle! Celery!

# CY came to PARTYYY!!

C-Y came to party
Together they sound like see
Icy! Fancy! Bouncy! Mercy! Juicy!
C-Y get on the floor
And bring your friends to party some more
Icy, Spicy, Legacy, Urgency!

# E and D!!

My name is E-D
You add me to the end
I'm something like magic
Let's make pretend
I change words once
the action happens
You can be the captain
if you feel my rapping
Take the word walk
Add me and it becomes walked
Take the word talk
Add me and it becomes talked

# WR!!

*Meet WR*

I'm the best writer on the block

You can tell by the way I hold my chalk

I **wr**eck the pen and paper

It's all in the **wr**ist game

I know that the w doesn't say his name

I wrote all my poems using w-r words

I bet you can't use em like me

**Wr**ench (leg tap)

**Wr**ong (leg tap)

**Wr**inkle (leg tap)

# Who is PH??

Teacher! Teacher!

I think I need some help

Let me know what the word begins with

So I can help myself

Frog he said F

Phone he said P-H

Photo he said P-H

Fish he said F

Philip he said P-H

# Let me tell you about my best friend TH!!

T-H is my best friend

I see him every day

Here are some words

So you can see him play

**Th**eodore, **th**ermostat, **th**roat

**Th**at, **th**is, **th**ere, **th**ump

**Th**row, **th**umb, **th**read

# L-Y sounds like LEEEEEE!!

L-Y sounds like LEE

The girl sat quiet-LY

Her brother cried loud-LY

The dog ran quick-LY

The bird chirped proud-LY

I just learned how to use l-y correct-LY

**Meet: The "Magic E" or "Silent E" or the "Bossy E"**

# Magic E sounds like SILENCE!!

Meet the *magic e*. He hides at the end of words.

If we have the word sit, it sounds like this for each letter→sss /iiii /ttt. What kind of "i" do we hear in the word sit? We hear a short "i." Great! However, if we add an e to the word, the "i" will become a long vowel and produce the long "i" instead of the short "i." The word then becomes site.

**Examples of Magic E Words**

Bike – between the vowels there is a consonant. We have the vowel i, followed by a consonant, and then the silent e.

| Consonant | Vowel | Consonant |
|-----------|-------|-----------|
| i | k | e |

When we sound out bike, we hear the "i" sound in its name, but do we hear the "e?" **Noooooo**.

The e has become a *magic e*. It makes the previous vowel (i) say its name and become a *long* vowel.

Try sounding out these magic e words. (T<u>i</u>me, v<u>o</u>te, l<u>i</u>ne, l<u>a</u>te, p<u>i</u>le, f<u>i</u>ne, c<u>a</u>pe, l<u>a</u>ke, n<u>i</u>ne, h<u>i</u>de)

Ask your student: Does the letter in midnight blue make a long vowel sound by saying its name? (The answer is yes).

Write here what you think below or in your journal.

# Meet this Digraph

*IE sounds like IIIIII!!*

Here we have a vowel team[1]!

Let's talk about the word p<u>ie</u>. As noticed, the vowel team in the word pie is "ie." Now, sound out the word. Do you hear the p sound? Yes. Great. Do you hear the "i?" Yes. You do? What kind of "i" do you hear? A long vowel? Great. Do you hear the "E?" Nope? Great. We can hear the "i" say its name(long vowel), but the "E" vowel is silent.

*Sound out the words below, color the long vowel sound you hear, and underline the silent vowel next to the long vowel.*

| LIE | UNTIE | DRIED | REPLIED |
| --- | --- | --- | --- |
| CRIED | SPIED | TIED | FRIES |
| DIE | TIE | TRIED | PIE |

---

[1] Two vowels side by side, but the first vowel sound is present while the second vowel sound is silent.

Can you try to find 7 more words around the house that use the **ie vowel team**?

Spelling sound or Rule of the week

_____

Give an example of the spelling sound or rule of the week below

_____

Directions: Write a silly story that has a beginning, middle, and ending using a few *magic e* words that you know

_____

_____

_____

_____

_____

_____

_____

Draw a cool picture to go with your writing (*from the previous page*) in the box below.

Choose any sounds covered in the book from poems or activity pages.

Write a spelling sound or rule of the week

**Insert notes or reminders here:**

Directions: Write a story about an inventor using a few _____ *(reinsert sound of the week here)* words that you found around your home. If you need more space, write the rest in your journal.

_____

_____

_____

_____

_____

_____

_____

Draw a scene to go with your story.

Hey friends. Meet Nasir. He wants to save money for new sneakers. For each word Nasir gets $10.00. Help Nasir reach his goal by writing *magic e* words next to the dollar sign.

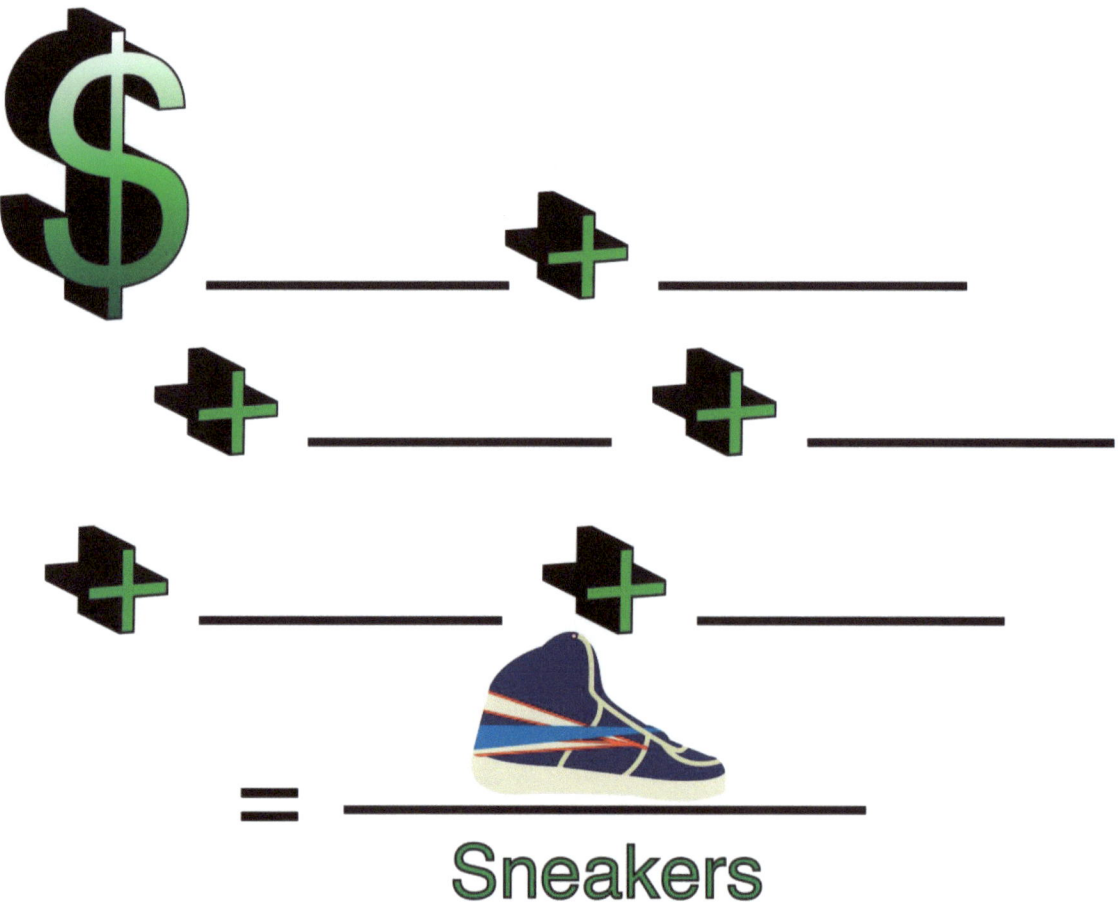

*Cha! Ching! Thank you for helping Nasir reach his goal.*
*Hard work pays off! Keep it up!*

# Meet this Diphthong[2]

*AI sounds like AAAAAAA!!*

A vowel team is when we find two vowels side by side, but you hear the first vowel sound while the second vowel remains silent.

Take the word rain for instance. "AI" is the vowel team present in this particular word.

Now let's sound out the word rain. Do you hear the "r?" Yes. Do you hear the "a" (long vowel)? Yes. Do you hear the "i?" Nope. Now, can you hear the "n"? Great. The "a" is heard, but the "i" is not. Great work.

*Sound out the words below, color the long vowel sound you hear, and underline (or place a star over it) the silent vowel next to the long vowel. *Reminder vowels are a,e,i,o,u. Example:   Rain*

| WAIT | RAIN | TRAIN | CLAIM |
|------|------|-------|-------|
| SNAIL | RAIL | RAINY | GAIN |
| TAIL | PAIL | BRAINY | MAIN |

Draw 2 pictures to accompany your favorite AI word below.

---

[2] A sound formed by the combination of two vowels in a single syllable, in which the sound begins as one vowel and moves toward another.

# Can you score with me?

**Purpose**: The purpose of this game is to allow children to practice saying specific vowel sounds while having fun scoring goals.

**Directions**: Grab two or three wastebaskets. Pick 2 or 3 vowel teams or spelling sounds from the book. Write on a few squares to show the chosen "sounds of the day." Tape these squares to the front of the baskets you have. Write 3-7 words on the back of the basket that go with the ONE sound on the front.

### Playing Time (1 or more players)

Have players take turns sitting in front of the rows of buckets. Hold the paper ball in hand. *Player must say the "sound of the day"* on the front of the basket and do a hand gesture like punching the air or a double clap. They can also sing a poem from the workbook that matches the sound.

*Shoot the ball into a basket.* Then run to the back of the basket and read the word out loud. The next player takes his or her turn. Shoot the ball into the basket. Play until all baskets and words have been used or read.

Here are a few suggested sounds to study. Just write the sound on the front and write words on the back of the basket that match the sound. *Students can refer to notebooks or poems to assist them with pronunciation.

| EA | OU | OW |
|---|---|---|
| leaf, bead, beak, please, neat | loud, sound, house, shout, pout, pound | now, howl, cow, owl, town |
| AW | AI | QU |
| jaw, straw, law, draw, raw, paw, saw, flaw | brain, snail, mail, drain, aim, chain | queen, quiz, equal, quarter, quiet |
| IE | EE | STR |
| pie, die, dried, tie, fries, lie, lied | knee, three, degree, sweet, meet, teeth | straight, strong, street, strap, string |

 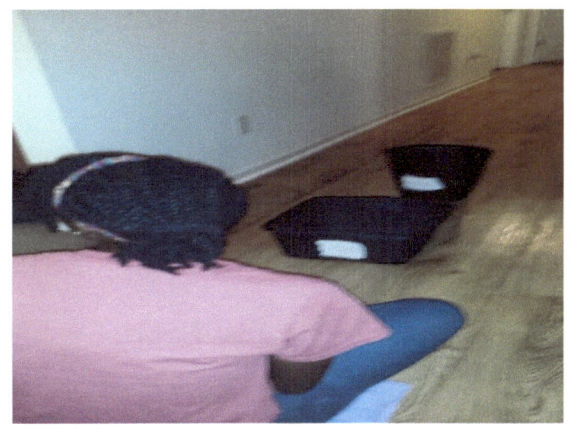

Front*

Back *

# Meet Vowel Teams

*OA sounds like OOOOOOO!!*

We have two vowels side by side, but **the first vowel says its name (long vowel) and the second vowel is silent!**

The word for today is "goat!" The vowel team is oa. Now, sound out the word with me. Great job! Do you hear the g? Yes. Do you hear the "o" (long vowel)? Yes. Do you hear the "a?" Nope. Can you hear the "t?" Yes. Great. We can hear the "O" sound, but the "A" sound is silent.

*Slowly sound out the words below, color the long vowel sound you hear, and underline the silent sound on the right next to the long vowel.*

| GOAT | COAT | BOAT | LOAD | LOAF |
|------|------|------|------|------|
| FLOAT | ROAD | BONE (exemption- draw a picture) | SOAP | CONE (exemption- draw a picture) |

*Bone and cone do not contain the vowel pair OA. However, what vowel sound do you hear loud and clear? The *o* sound. Great thinking. *Parents you can have students write response in their journal so they don't always see the answer in responses in the book.

_____

Our words are quite lonely. Can you try to put a few of them into sentences? Try to create two sentences.

_____

_____

Record notes and ideas below (parent or student):

# EA sounds like EEEEEE!!

A vowel team is when we find **two vowels side by side within a word, but the first vowel says its name and the second vowel is silent.**

Let's examine the word "beach" to find the vowel diagraph. Ea is our vowel digraph. Sound out the word beach. Hear the "b?" Yes. Awesome! Hear the "e" (long vowel)? Yes. Hear the "a?" No! Hear the "C" and "H?" Yes!

In the word beach, we can hear the "E" sound, but the "A" sound is silent.

*Slowly sound out the words below, color the long vowel sound you hear, and underline the sound on the right next to the long vowel.*

| CL<u>E</u>AN | SEA | BEAT | TEACH |
|---|---|---|---|
| FLEA | REACH | PLEASE | EACH |

My words are quite lonely; can you find 3 more words in a few books that use this vowel team?

Write them in your journal. Try to write a sentence with each word you find.

# EE sounds like EEEEEEE!!

When you can **hear the first vowel, but not the second vowel in a duo of vowels**, it is called a vowel team.

When it comes to the double "E," we hear a long vowel "E".

Beep, deep, creek. What's common in all of these words is the long "E" sound present within the middle of the word.

Let's examine "creek" a little closer. When saying the word, you're able to hear all the letters, but the double "E" stands out.

*Read each word below.*

- *Day 1-Underline the vowel team as you say the sound.*
- *Day 2 -Pick 4 words and write it 4 times.*
- *Day 3- Pick 2 words and draw small pictures to represent the words.*
- *Day 4- Write a poem in your journal using 3 of these words.*

sheep _____

keep _____

creek _____

feed _____

beef _____

bees _____

*There's a new team in town. Watch out!*

# OU sounds like OWWWWWW!!

*As in OUCHHHH*

**"OU" and "OW" make the same sound most of the time.**

Say H<u>OU</u>SE. Now say GR<u>OW</u>L. Do you hear the ouuu sound?

- *Activity Time*
    - *Please unscramble the words below.*
    - *Highlight the "OU or OW" in each word in a bright color.*
    - *Write a story about fictional computers, grocery stores or kid scientist with the "OW" words in your journal.*

1. wot _____
2. spuot _____
3. glrow _____
4. dhonu_____
5. woh_____
6. rwo_____
7. wos_____
8. olw _____

# OO

**"OO" can be used to represent different sounds such as in "C-OO-L" or as in "F-OO-T." As a reader, when you have to decide which "OO" sound fits the word, you are reading.**

Use "OO" as a starting point. *Add* new consonants and vowels *as needed* to create new words.

1. Write oo on a line. 2. Choose a initial sound, blend or digraph.

3. Add the blend to your word. Example: SHOO __ 4. Choose an ending sound. Example: SHOOT

Feel free to look through a few of your books to get ideas!

| Individual Letters *Add extra letters as needed | M | S | E | L | K | N | F | B | R | W | D | T | C |
|---|---|---|---|---|---|---|---|---|---|---|---|---|---|

| Blends & Digraphs | SH | PR | TH | GL | SP | BR | CH | SM |
|---|---|---|---|---|---|---|---|---|

| Shoot | | |
|---|---|---|
| | | |
| | | |

# Meet the Friendly Team!!

**"AW" and "AU"**

The friendly team refers to <u>two letters brought together in order to act as one vowel sound.</u>

We can also spell this sound two different ways. Ex. s**AW** & s**AU**ce

*Activity*

Let's help out Mariah! Mariah needs to complete her text messages on her cell phone.

Use the word bank inside the battery to fill in the sentences. Pay attention to the aw and au sounds you may see. Good luck.

*Cellphone*  *Battery*

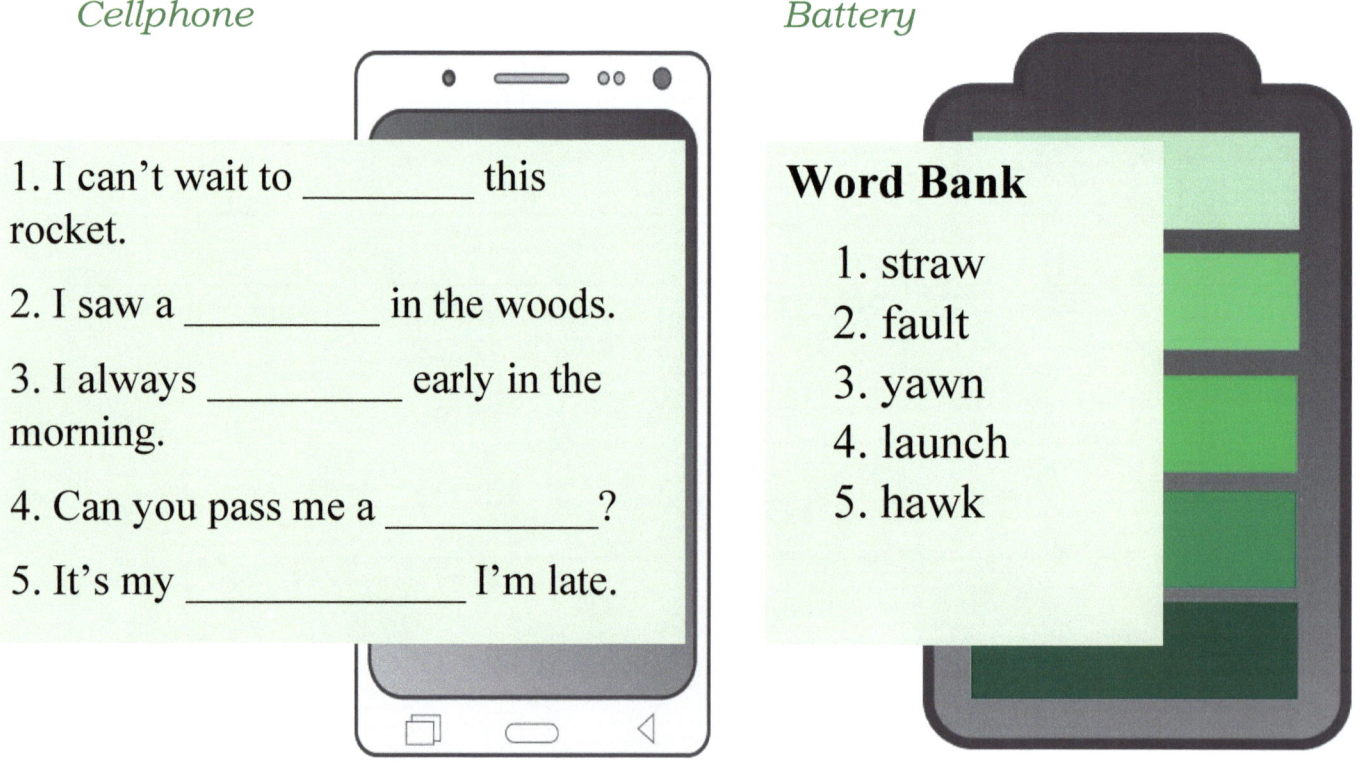

1. I can't wait to _____ this rocket.
2. I saw a _____ in the woods.
3. I always _____ early in the morning.
4. Can you pass me a _____?
5. It's my _____ I'm late.

**Word Bank**
1. straw
2. fault
3. yawn
4. launch
5. hawk

# Meet the Tricky Team!!

**"EY" & "AY"**

Let's work through some words.

TRAY. What sounds does "TR" sound make? It sounds like *Truuhhh*.

What does the "AY" sound make? It sounds like both "EY" and "AY" even though the spelling is reflected as "AY."

Marcus and Leon are having an action figure fight on their favorite video game. Help Marcus's character win by filling up his controller with the juice. In order to get enough juice to win he needs some new "AY" words. Help Leon's character win by filling up his controller with the juice. He needs some new "EY" words.

Write the words *under* the heading neatly to help both character come out on top!

# Consonant Cluster

*A consonant cluster is a pair or thrice[3] of consonants (letters that are NOT vowels) that are grouped together in order to make a sound.*

For example, spl- sounds like splu. We use it in words such as: spl-ash, spl-at, spl-inter, spl-endid, spl-atter!

Try choosing a word of the day from the boxes below and write it in your journal. Look at each side of the word and sound out exactly what you see. Do these sounds remind you of any other words you know? Talk about it with a friend. Try doing this twice a day for 7 days.

| | | | | | | |
|---|---|---|---|---|---|---|
| **SPL** | | | split | | | |
| **SP** | | sprinkle | | spray | | |
| **STR** | | strawberry | | stranger | | street |
| **CL** | clean | | clean | | closet | closest |
| **SM** | smell | | small | smoke | smash | smoothie |
| **TW** | twin | | two | twinkle | twice | twenty | twist |

## Optional Activities

Day 1-2 Have your child choose a consonant cluster from the **boxes above** for the *day*. Write a few words with that sound in pencil in your child's journal. Have the student trace over the cluster sound in crayon.

---

[3] Three times, as in succession; on three occasions or in three ways.

Have students practice saying the cluster sound repeatedly as they trace it in crayon.

Day 3-5 You can also grab Elmer's glue. Write the cluster of the day in glue on a small poster or sheet of construction paper. Have the child place dry kidney beans on the glue to spell out the cluster of the day. Ask the student to write six words around the beans and glue that match the cluster.

Day 5-9 It is imperative that students write sentences and paragraphs with the sounds of the day to become comfortable with consonant clusters in their journals.

Students or parents can write notes or memos below.

# Game Time using Consonant Clusters!

Myia challenged Ricky to a basketball game. Fill up the lines on the right using words that have the "sm" sound at the beginning for Myia. Fill up the lines on the right that have the "cl" sound at the beginning for Ricky. Play with a friend to see who wins!

**_Team Myia_**                                                         **_Team Ricky_**

_____    **2 points**    _____

_____    **3 points**    _____

_____    **4 points**    _____

_____    **5 points**    _____

# Let's fix this broken ladder!

A storm left tremendous damage in Anthony's hometown. He decided to help his father repair several roofs in his neighborhood. As Anthony stood on top of the roof, a strong wind came. The wooden ladder fell. Oh no! The ladder broke in half. Help Anthony repair the broken ladder by writing words that have the ai, ee, ea, or oo on the blank spaces.

# Dance Battle

Roger loves to show off his dance moves. I bet you do too. Help Roger cover the blank spaces on this dance floor with words that have an AU or OU sound. For each word you do or find with a friend hit a dance move. That's right. Shake or shout after you have covered a square with an au or ou word!

Have your child or student highlight the vowel in each dance square. Say the vowel sound to your family. Ask them to guess which vowel sound you are saying.

Example: Your student writes the word *sauce* on a square. They will then sound out the "au" vowel sound ignoring the other letters. Allow them to ask family members which vowel sound they think he or she is using. After two tries he/she will display the mystery word on a dry erase board. He/she will underline the vowel they wanted the family to hear. S<u>au</u>ce.

*Congrats. Thank you for helping Roger to win. After sounding out vowels, grab the music and have a dance competition with a friend.*

# What is Meaning?

*And the strategies to help.*

*Strategies can be stretched over 2-3 days.

Meaning can be defined as what is expressed by a word or concept. Readers make meaning when they fully understand what they are reading.

**Pre-reading**

**Strategy 1:** When students receive a new book, they should practice scanning the book. *Scanning is when students read the title and glance over each page.* As they closely look at the pictures, they try to quickly read at least one phrase on each page.

Script: Hey, we have a new book. Let's read the title together. Now, let's practice scanning this book. I want you to flip through each page. I don't want you to read it word for word. Let's just read one phrase on each page and look at the pictures. What do you see on these different pages? Allow the student to respond. What do you notice about the pictures on each page? Allow student to respond.

*Activity:* Let's write 5 sentences about what we think we will learn from this book in our journal. Use the words **"I predict"** to illustrate each of those thoughts.

Let's draw a tiny race car in the box by each of our predictions if we found them to be true after we read the whole story.

- Example
  - ☐ I predict this book will give me information about werewolves.
  - ☐ I predict this book will teach me about the rules of a soccer game.
  - ☐ I predict this book will be about how to make a paper airplane.

**Strategy 2:** Reread the longer parts. As our students advance their reading level, the books that they read will become longer. An effective reader rereads the longer parts to help them make stronger connections, i.e. themes, plot, setting, character analysis, etc.

<u>Script:</u> Hey, how do you feel about this book? Allow students to share. Well, good readers love to read longer parts 2 times. Reading the story more than once makes our brains stronger and our reading levels progress at a faster rate.

Option 1: Sketch what you are visualizing.

Option 2:

Based on what you read, if you were a teacher what lesson would you teach from this book? Respond in your journal or below.

*Once strategies have been practiced in this book, please keep practicing daily. It is expected the strategy be repeated in the personal student's journal daily. All strategies are very crucial to each reader's success.

*Some strategies can take place over 2-3 days depending on the length of the book.

Parent script:

Day 1: The first time we read the book, I will give you one minute to draw a picture about everything you learned. You are going to

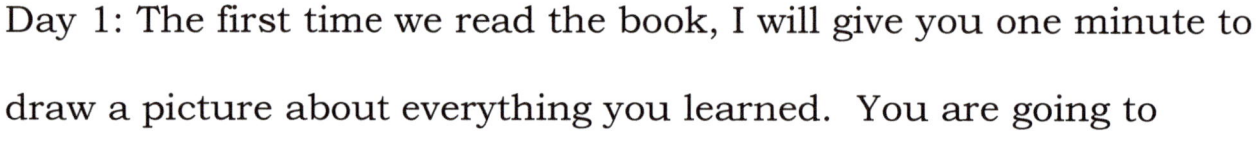

pretend this picture is for your favorite singer, actress, athlete, inventor or friend. You will have to teach them everything you learned using your drawing.

Parent Script: Day 2: The second time we read the book; I will give you two minutes to write 10 words across the page that this book was all about. Make sure the words are neat. Pretend you are writing these words to help teach younger students all about this book. Write the words below or in your journal.

_____

_____

<u>Script:</u> Day 3: Now we've read the book twice! Great work. You are a real reader. Let's read the book one more time. Once we are done, I will give you three minutes to write captions under the "word-ful" pictures you will create. Choose two words from your list above. Place the word in the box. Decorate the word within the box. Write a detailed sentence about the word you chose to represent your book.

[ ]

_____

_____

[ ]

_____

*Reminder. Once the previous pages are filled. Students should complete the same strategy with new books in their journal.

**Strategy 4**

Listen up parents/tutors. This is where you change roles. You are going to be the student. Your child/student is going to be the teacher. You are going to select a book your child/student can read. You will read it to them, but you are going to read one word on each page incorrectly (picture books are encouraged).

*Why, you may ask?* The purpose of doing so is to prompt your child to correct you and give you a reason or strategy to help you get it right the next time.

Script: Hey, are you ready for a new book? Great. Let's read this book together. It's been a while since I've read it, but I want you to help me fix the words I get wrong. Let's try it with the title.

Parent: I like to sww—swamp. Text says "I like to swim."

Student: Hey, that's not swamp!

Parent: But the beginning sound is sw.

Student: But look at the picture. The picture shows a little boy swimming.

Parent: Oh okay. The word is swimming.

Student: It can't be swimming. It's too long. Student takes finger and sounds out the words. Swwiiimmm. Swim.

You may want to practice this with your child several times before starting your *official* lesson. By allowing your child to become the teacher, they will develop their ability to correct you and themselves while reading. We don't want our readers to read over words incorrectly and keep pushing. We want them to automatically work through the incorrectness and correct it every time!!!

Once you have used the pages for this activity, you can allow the child to complete the same strategies in their journal.

## Record notes and ideas below (parent or student):

# What is Writing?

**Writing is a form of written expression.**

**Strategy 1:** Have students **bold** the beginning letter of all sentences. Bolding the first letter will remind them to make sure the first letter is capital.

Script: Hey, when we are writing complete sentences in this notebook lets practice bolding the beginning letter in each sentence. You can use a crayon or a pencil. I think it will help us remember to capitalize the beginning of each sentence. Write 2-3 sentences about your favorite subject, hobby, sibling, movie, car, game or holiday.

**Strategy 2:** Changing sounds to make new words. I want you to select a base word. Once you choose a base word for the week, practice changing that base word to several new words daily.

Script: Hey. We are going to choose a "base" word and make new word. Are you ready to hear the rules?

I want you to pick a base word and then we are going to make it with the magnetic letters.

You picked the word *move* great! Let's make it.

*Base words are located on the next page.

**Example 1**

Step 1—M O V E

Step 2—(Script)—I wonder if we change one or two letters, what new word can we make? Let's try one letter. Let's add the letter s. What word do we have now?

M O V E S

Step 3—(Script)—I wonder if we take off the e and s and add an i and e, what word we will have?

M O V E S will then become M O V I E.

Script: Can we hear the "I" in this word? No.

What vowel can we hear? We hear the long "E."

**Example 2**

Step 1—C U P

Step 2—(Script)—I wonder what new words we can make with cup?

What letter or letters would you like to move around?

Want to add an "S?" Let's do it!

C U P S

Step 3—(Script)—I wonder what other words we could make if we take off the "P" and the "S."

What sound does "CU" make? Cuh.

How could we make the word cute?

We need to add a "t" and a "e."

C U T E. Fantastic job!!

*Try it out . Use the bold words in the first column as base words. Try to prompt your student to see what letters are needed to build the words in the next column. ***Keep these words covered.**

Parent script: Our base word is blue. Hmm. I wonder what letters we could add to make blues…Great! You said an s. I wonder what letters we could switch around to make sue?

| **Mouse** | house | houses | louse |
|---|---|---|---|
| **Sand** | hand | man | band |
| **Nail** | jail | tail | rail |

| **Move** | moves | movies | moving |
| --- | --- | --- | --- |
| **Blue** | blues | sue | glue |
| **Swim** | swam | swing | swat |
| **Cross** | crosses | boss | loss |
| **Car** | cars | bar | bars |
| **Swoosh** | swim | swamp | switch |
| **Light** | lights | bright | sight |
| **Lake** | bake | cake | care |
| **Sit** | lit | bit | bite |
| **Black** | blank | blood | blur |

- Optional words to try as needed. Try these words as base word. And ask your child to start with the base word. You will want your student to remove beginning sounds and ending sounds in order to create new words.
    - Broom
    - Grass
    - Few
    - No
    - Wall
    - Food
    - Dish

Focus on one base word for a week. After you have created a new word, write 5 sentences in a silly poem using those words.

**For example:**

Jessica loved to play in the **sand** (base word).

Then she joined a band.

I hope she made at least a grand.

Dear Jessica, please give me a hand!

*You can take away one, two, or three letters as needed to make a new word. You can add one, two, or three letters as needed to make a new word. We want children to see that they can find <u>sounds</u> they already know in larger words. When you run out of words to make, create the base word again. Then start working with the ending or beginning and attempting another approach. You can ask the child hey what letters do we need to change this word into this word? Allow the student to move the magnetic letters around on a refrigerator or use a dry erase maker to cross out letters you don't want to use anymore.*

**Strategy 3:** Punctuation marks. Write a sentence using a word of the day with each punctuation mark.

Example: I heard the baby cry.  Do puppies cry like babies? Do not cry about the spilled milk!

Periods (.) are used to complete a simple sentence.

Question marks (?) are used to ask about something.

Exclamation marks (!) are used to make a loud statement.

Record notes and ideas below (parent or student):

# Author's Introduction

My name is Patrice A. Barrett; I was born in 1990 in Brooklyn, New York, but I was raised and lived in both Gifford and Allendale, South Carolina. I graduated from Estill High School as the 2009 Valedictorian and throughout my high school career I participated in the JROTC, Teacher Cadet, and Teaching Fellow programs. I graduated from Winthrop University with a bachelor's degree in Early Childhood. I then graduated from the University of South Carolina with a Master of Arts in Language and Literacy. Everything in me has a true passion for literacy. Growing up, I wanted to teach children how to read. Hearing various students read aloud in class without fluency brought me to this idea. I wanted to develop a tool parents and/or tutors could use over the years to help our students further develop their reading skills. Enjoy! ☺

Bibliography

Drawception. (2017). *Broken ladder.* Retrieved from

https://drawception.com/panel/drawing/MTDs3336/broken-ladder/

Easy Drawing. (2016, Apr 25). *How to draw a basketball.* Retrieved from

https://www.youtube.com/watch?v=UHIoA_GJVtI

King, J. (2014). *How to draw a good enough video game controller.* Retrieved from

http://jeannelking.com/dev/draw-good-enough-video-game-controller/

Krache, D. (2012, June 20). *By the numbers: high school dropouts.* Retrieved from

http://schoolsofthought.blogs.cnn.com/2012/06/20/by-the-numbers-high-school-

dropouts/

O'Neil, D. (2006, Aug. 31). *What is language?* Retrieved from

http://anthro.palomar.edu/language/language_2.htm

Reading Partners. (2013, Oct. 7). *Do prisons use third grade reading scores to predict the

number of prison beds they'll need?* Retrieved from http://readingpartners.org/blog/do-

prisons-use-third-grade-reading-scores-to-predict-the-number-of-prison-beds-theyll-

need/

Slimber. (2017). *Dance floor.* Retrieved from http://slimber.com/gallery/image/dance-

floor:g111738.html

Sparks, S. (2011, Apr. 8). *Study: third grade reading predicts later high school graduation.*

Retrieved from http://blogs.edweek.org/edweek/inside-school-

research/2011/04/the_disquieting_side_effect_of.html